Brontë Country

The Parsonage, Haworth

Brontë Country

Edited by Glenda Leeming

Photographs by Simon Warner and Howard Beck

Brian Trodd Publishing House

Published in UK by
Brian Trodd Publishing House Limited
27 Swinton St, London WC1

Printed in the Canary Islands   Lito. A. Romero, S. A. - D. L. TF. 303 – 1988

ISBN 1 85361 002 X

Remote farmhouse near Ponden Clough, Haworth Moor.

Acknowledgements

All photographs are by Simon Warner except for the following, which are by Howard Beck: pp. 4-5, 7, 11, 12, 26, 36, 37, 40-41, 50-51, 60, 63, 64-65, 74, 79, 94, 102-103, 114, 118-119, 121.

The portrait of the Brontë sisters (back jacket) by Branwell Brontë is reproduced by permission of the National Portrait Gallery.

Contents

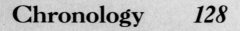

Foreword

by The Rt Hon Roy Hattersley, MP

Charlotte, Emily and Anne Brontë were, for all their wild, timeless genius, unmistakably the product of nineteenth century Yorkshire. They wrote about strange vices and improbable virtues which Haworth village and Keighley, in the valley below, never knew. Novels as great as theirs should not be diminished by adjectives which pretend that their appeal is regional or their values less than universal, but the background to their stories is always the high ground of the West Riding.

The moors around Wuthering Heights and Thornfield Hall ('ripe bilberries gleaming here and there like jet beads') are the moors which run across the Pennines. And the rain ('like spray sometimes sharp like shot') which swept through *Villette* is not a Belgian storm but a Yorkshire squall. The stone houses are the millstone grit manors and the slabbed roof farmhouses of the families who made their livings from the rough grazing at the top of the dales.

The essentially Yorkshire detail in *Wuthering Heights* worried Charlotte about the reception which her sister's novel was likely to receive from southern readers to whom 'the natural characteristics of the outlying hills and hamlets in the West Riding of Yorkshire are things alien and unfamiliar... The wild moors of the north of England can for them have no interest.' Charlotte was of course wrong, as Mrs Gaskell was wrong when she arrived at Keighley station to begin her research for her biography of the author of *Jane Eyre* and found the area so unattractive that she feared a stranger could never come to understand it.

It is, of course, hard country – grey in winter and dark green even in spring. The grass in the fields is sharp and the bracken and heather on the hills is tough enough to survive the moorland winter. It is the right sort of place for Lowood Institution, and boarding schools for chronically unwanted children abounded in the area. Up the road at Greta Bridge, Mr Wackford Squeers founded Dotheboys Hall. But it is also proud – indeed, heroic – country. It is a place for sins not peccadillos, desperate love not flippant infatuation, not sadness but despair.

But it is country in which even Catherine and Heathcliff found peace and which inspired their incomparable epitaph:

'I lingered round them, under that benign sky, watched the moths fluttering among the heath and harebells, listened to the soft wind breathing through the grass, and wondered how any one could ever imagine unquiet slumbers for the sleepers in that quiet earth.'

Charlotte, Emily and Anne Brontë's novels are now read throughout the English-speaking world but it is not just the beauty and power of their books that have made them so popular. Their tragically short lives, so similar to many of the characters in their novels, have excited their readers' imagination. Charlotte's friend and biographer, Mrs. Gaskell, was only the first to comment on the sisters' solitary existence and to feel the attraction of the 'sinuous wave-like hills', crowned with heather, that surround Haworth —

> grand, from the ideas of solitude and loneliness which they suggest, or oppressive from the feeling which they give of being pent-up by some monotonous and illimitable barrier, according to one's mood.

But, as she also remarked, perhaps these wild bleak moors were also essential to their inspiration — a softer climate might have improved their health without nourishing their peculiar genius. The relationship of the Brontës to their surroundings is still fascinating to anyone who goes to the village of Haworth: the isolation of Haworth Parsonage conjures up scenes from a self-contained drama. Even though Haworth in the nineteenth century was fairly close to busy manufacturing areas, its local moors, wild and bleak as Mrs. Gaskell found them, were extensive enough to separate the Brontë children from comparable families. So they grew up to feel that it was easier to enjoy mutual understanding and shared tastes within the family than to make the effort of adapting to the rare outsider; and they also grew to love the power and stark beauty of the moors that surrounded them.

However, the use that the Brontë sisters made of this scenery in their works is not quite as straightforward as it seems. In their novels they evoked pictures reminiscent of Haworth and its moors, but many of these, possibly all, are 'composed' scenes that mingle different elements. For instance, Charlotte may have remembered the countryside around Cowan Bridge in North Lancashire, where she, Emily and their two elder sisters were sent to school. While at school, the elder sisters Maria and Elizabeth became ill and they returned home to die sometime later. Charlotte's bitterness at her sisters' deaths burnt the experience into her memory, and her savage description of Lowood in *Jane Eyre* is based upon the school. However, she was only eight when she went there, and her impression of the woods, stream and remoter hills must owe much to her personal vision, drawing its sources from Haworth and elsewhere.

All artists mingle experience and imagination, and the various transformations of the Yorkshire moors were a major inspiration for the budding writers. As the little Brontës grew up together at Haworth — because it was some time before another outside school was risked — the fantasy sagas of their active imaginations incorporated their well-loved surroundings. Angria, the fantasy country shared by Charlotte with her brother Branwell, is nominally in Africa, but when she writes of Angria, it is her native Yorkshire that gives shape and substance to her imaginary country.

> Sometimes I have filled the air with the whitened tempest of winter: snow has embossed the dark arms of the beech and oak and filled with drifts the parks of the lowlands or the mountain-pass of wilder districts. Again the same mansion with its woods, the same moor with its glens, has been softly coloured with the tints of moonlight in summer . . .

Likewise, in the poems dealing with Gondal, evolved by Emily and Anne, snow, heather and larks are familiar elements.

As they grew up, the Brontë sisters developed different feelings about their home and its background. Charlotte was the most outgoing of the three. She had a considerable curiosity about the rest of the world and

The Brontë Parsonage and Sunday School in the village of Haworth.

envied friends who were able to travel. When opportunities to travel did arise she always wanted her sisters to share in her experience. Certainly her second experience of school, at Miss Wooler's establishment, was more successful than her first, in spite of homesickness. But when she returned there as a teacher, taking first Emily, then Anne, to be educated free in return for her labours, her younger sisters were not able to thrive or at least endure as Charlotte could. Later it was Charlotte who initiated the plan for herself and Emily to spend time in a Belgian school, qualifying themselves to set up a school of their own at the parsonage. Later still, as a successful author, Charlotte was happy to accept invitations to stay or travel with friends and acquaintances: she recalled her first reactions to visiting the Lake District, 'a glorious region – of which I had only seen the similitude in dreams – waking or sleeping. . . .' Charlotte's tastes seem to have been quite flexible, for while the Lake District and Scotland offer the same kind of scenery as Yorkshire, her enthusiasm for the totally different, flat, Belgian landscape is

Norton Conyers, near Ripon. Charlotte Brontë stayed here and legend claims that a mad woman was locked into the upper rooms of the house. Perhaps this was the source of inspiration for the character of Mrs. Rochester in Jane Eyre.

more surprising. However, her feelings for M. Heger, husband of her headmistress in Belgium (speculated on by generations of biographers though never admitted by Charlotte herself), possibly explain her attachment to the Belgian countryside, as well as her subsequent dissatisfaction with her home. 'There was a time when Haworth was a very pleasant place to me; it is not so now. I feel as if we were all buried here.'

Emily and Anne however, were much happier at Haworth than elsewhere. They were sufficient to each other, and did not make friends at school as Charlotte did. To Emily, the moors around Haworth were not imprisonment but freedom. Even the removal to Miss Wooler's school in another part of Yorkshire was intolerable. Of her stay, Charlotte wrote:

My sister Emily loved the moors. Flowers brighter than the rose bloomed in the blackest heath for her; – out of a sullen hollow in a livid hill-side, her mind could make an Eden. She found in the bleak solitude many and dear delights; and not the least and best-loved was – liberty . . . Her nature proved here too strong for her fortitude. Every morning, when she woke, the vision of home and the moors rushed before her, and darkened and saddened the day that lay before her.

She was of course older when she went with Charlotte to Brussels, and was able to overcome a similar misery by sheer will power, but was 'never happy till she carried her hard-won knowledge back to the remote English village, the old parsonage-house, and the desolate Yorkshire hills'. Because of Emily's sufferings away from home, it was decided that after their aunt died, she should take over the running of the parsonage for their father, and even when her sisters left to go as governesses, she expressed a good deal of contentment in her diary papers, 'desiring that everybody could be as comfortable as myself and as undesponding', even in her monotonous life as housekeeper for the taciturn Mr Brontë.

Anne, though so like Emily, endured separation from home better – and she later remained at Thorpe Green as governess for four years, disliking it immensely. Charlotte claimed that her sisters had different preferences in their natural surroundings:

My sister Emily had a particular love for them (the moors) and there is not a knoll of heather, not a branch of fern, not a young bilberry leaf, not a fluttering lark or linnet, but reminds me of her. The distant prospects were Anne's delight, and when I look round she is in the blue tints, the pale mists, the waves and shadows of the horizon.

Anne was also deeply attracted to the sea, which she first visited with her employers. Later, almost immobilised by the last stages of tuberculosis, she retained a pathetic hope that a visit to Scarborough would do her good, and it was on this visit to the sea-side town that she died.

Top Withens on Haworth Moor, the site popularly associated with Wuthering Heights.

The novels are true to the Brontë sisters' experience in making the landscape and its changes of aspect an important part of the characters' lives. One of the most memorable features, of course, is their dramatic use of nature. Even Anne, whose descriptions are less frequent and more pedestrian than those of her sisters, unites the hero and heroine of *Agnes Grey* against a spectacular sunset sea-scape that no film director could improve upon. The lightning that ominously splits the chestnut tree beside which Rochester has just proposed to Jane Eyre, the storm into which Heathcliff disappears after hearing Catherine reject him, have a lurid vigour that perhaps derives from the Angrian and Gondal sagas. More realistically, Charlotte extends our understanding of the characters through the background to their lives. We first meet Jane Eyre looking out of the window at 'a pale blank of mist and cloud . . .

Looking towards Walshaw Dean from Alcomden Stones, Stanbury Moor.

wet lawn and storm-beat shrub, with ceaseless rain sweeping away wildly before a long and lamentable blast' – a suitable prospect for the orphaned, unloved child. Similarly, as Jane grows up, she looks out over distant hills, firstly from the school at Lowood, and later from the roof of Thornfield, Rochester's house, and longs for the freedom represented by the hills and their sense of unlimited space.

Nature expresses the feelings of the human characters, and Charlotte evokes whole landscapes to convey their state of mind. Jane's tranquil, charming but cold existence as a self-contained but inexperienced young woman is reflected in the wintry scene, when she sits on a stile beside the icy lane, 'whose best winter delight lay in its utter solitude and leafless repose . . . the stripped hawthorn and hazel bushes were as still as the white, worn stones which causewayed the middle of the path . . . the little brown birds which stirred occasionally in the hedge, looked like single russet leaves that had forgotten to drop.' Into this exquisite still-life, Charlotte Brontë brings the vigorous movement and sound of Rochester, a stranger on horseback, who is to interrupt Jane's tranquil life as he breaks into the scene of which she is a part.

More subtly, Charlotte uses Nature as a contrast too: when Jane runs away from Thornfield after her abortive wedding to Rochester, she has the feeling, familiar to most people at some time, that Nature is

indifferent or even critical of her personal struggle: 'I believe it was a lovely summer morning. . . . Birds began singing in brake and copse: birds were faithful to their mates; birds were emblems of love. What was I?' Both Jane and her creator have a strong sense of realism in their romanticism and though Jane seeks refuge alone among the great empty moors, she finds that unity with Nature has practical problems, such as hunger and cold. After her wandering in wild heathland, there is a beautiful little Constable-like picture, where nature incorporates a human element that reminds Jane of her inescapable ties to the rest of humanity:

. . . there, amongst the romantic hills, whose changes and aspect I had ceased to note an hour ago, I saw a hamlet and a spire. All the valley at my right hand was full of pasture-fields, and corn-fields, and wood; and a glittering stream ran zig-zag through the varied shades of green, the mellowing grain, the sombre wood-land, the clear and sunny lea. Recalled by the rumbling of wheels to the road before me, I saw a heavily-laden waggon labouring up the hill; and not far beyond were two cows and their drover. Human life and human labour were near. I must struggle on: strive to live and bend to toil like the rest.

The country neighbourhood that is the setting of *Shirley* is less romantic and more prosaic on the whole; the lanes, church, mill and villages have a solid, settled aspect. It is by the atmospheric effects of moonlight, storm, dawn, sunset, snow scenes and mist that these more mundane surroundings involve the reader in the feelings of the characters. Likewise, in *The Professor* and *Villette*, when the respective hero and heroine are mentally facing exile from England, the landscape reflects their disturbed feelings: Crimsworth in *The Professor* seeks out the sad but striking beauty of a winter sunset, 'glinting red through the leafless boughs of some very old oak trees', that he can both treasure and regret; Lucy Snowe in *Villette* more unusually observes 'a moving mystery – the Aurora Borealis', the 'northern lights' which are occasionally seen in northern England.

It is more difficult to find the human element in Emily Brontë's landscapes. The moors are always present in *Wuthering Heights* – they confuse the south-country narrator Lockwood, provide escape for the young Catherine and Heathcliff, and offer a meeting place for Catherine's daughter and Heathcliff's son. Otherwise there is little coming and going on everyday errands. Once away from the solitary houses and their fringe of pines or thorn trees, only the threatening crag or standing stone breaks the swell of the moorland.

Emily's character was 'not very flexible', 'unbending', as Charlotte put it, and the importance of stones and crags to one of her rock-like character is not unexpected. In the most famous speech in *Wuthering Heights* Catherine asserts 'My love for Heathcliff resembles the eternal rocks beneath: a source of little visible delight but necessary'. Charlotte in her introduction to the novel used the same imagery: '*Wuthering Heights* was hewn in a wild workshop, with simple tools, out of homely materials. The statuary found a granite block on a solitary moor; gazing thereon, he saw how from the crag might be elicited a head, savage, swart, sinister' – this head was Heathcliff's and the 'statuary' was Emily. It is difficult to imagine her using any other background but the moors, even if she had lived longer and written more. Apart from her personal attachment, the breadth and intensity of her imagination suited the background admirably. Moorland and heath have been used by certain writers for particular large scale effects – Shakespeare's King Lear cursing the storm on the heath springs to mind, and Hardy also sought the effect of superhuman brooding power in Egdon Heath in *The Return of the Native*. Only mountains, or the sea, can give such an effect of grandeur with the double power of either dwarfing or amplifying human emotions. Boldly, Emily forces us to respect the youthful feelings of Catherine and Heathcliff by relating them to the huge, intransigent landscape brooding in the background.

Like her sister, Emily could also manipulate her landscape with great subtlety. The close of *Wuthering Heights* is one of the most beautiful passages in the book – Lockwood muses on Catherine's and Heathcliff's graves:

I lingered round them under that benign sky, watched the moths fluttering among the heath and harebells, listened to the soft wind breathing through the grass, and wondered how any one could ever imagine unquiet slumbers for the sleepers in that quiet earth.

It seems the essence of peacefulness – but spoken by the imperceptive Lockwood, and remembering the context of the whole passion-racked story that has gone before, the tranquillity reverberates with that passion and with the irony of a 'quiet' that conceals the dangerous, volcanic and always threatening elements of life.

The sympathetic visitor to Haworth in particular and to the Yorkshire moors in general must feel something like this – Wuthering Heights is behind the next shoulder of moorland, Thornfield is hidden in the fold of hills beyond the dale, Angria and Gondal tremble behind the outlines of crag and fell. Though every reader's Wuthering Heights is his or her own, it is from this *kind* of landscape, with its specifically north country scale, perspective, colouring and quality of light, that the Brontë sisters realised the unique world and atmosphere of their novels.

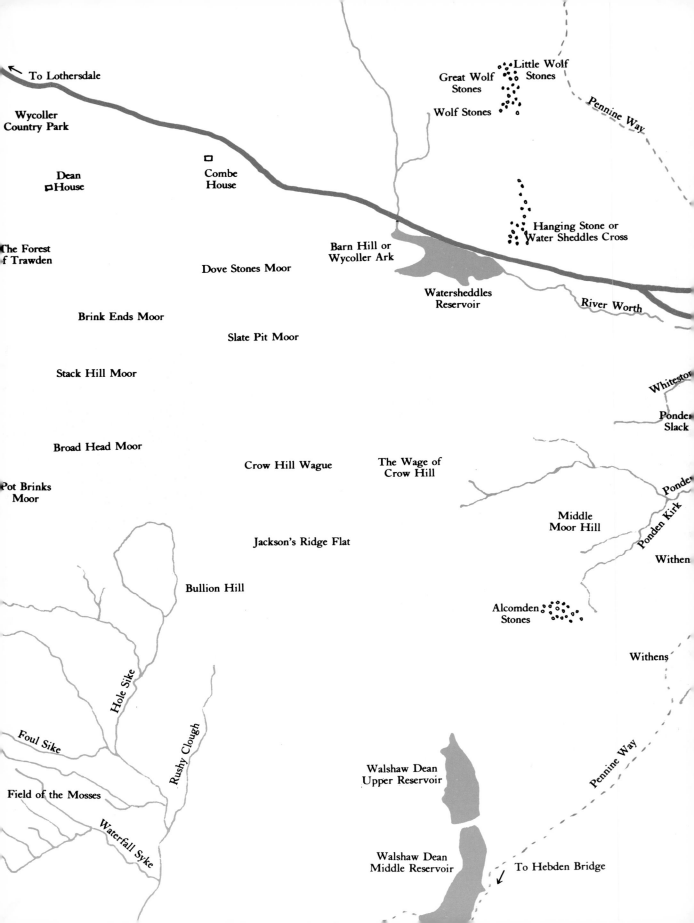

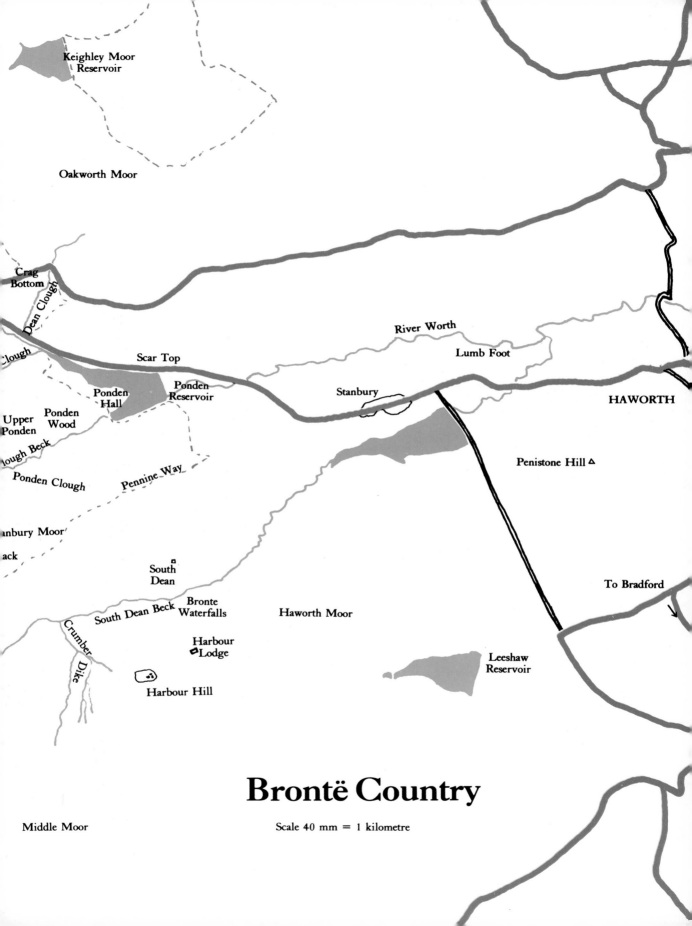

Keighley Moor
Reservoir

Oakworth Moor

Crag
Bottom

Dean Clough

Clough

River Worth

Scar Top

Lumb Foot

Ponden
Reservoir

Stanbury

HAWORTH

Ponden
Hall

Upper
Ponden

Ponden
Wood

Penistone Hill △

lough Beck

Ponden Clough

Pennine Way

anbury Moor

ack

South
Dean

To Bradford

South Dean Beck

Bronte
Waterfalls

Haworth Moor

Crumber Dike

Harbour
Lodge

Leeshaw
Reservoir

Harbour Hill

Brontë Country

Middle Moor

Scale 40 mm = 1 kilometre

Moorland

Previous page: The heather in full bloom on
Haworth Moor.

Most of the characters in the Brontë novels are natives of the moors and are deeply attached to
their homes, like the Rivers sisters in *Jane Eyre*, who seem to be based on Emily and Anne.

*They clung to the purple moors behind and around their dwelling — to
the hollow vale into which the pebbly bridle-path leading from their
gate descended, and which wound between fern-banks first, and then
amongst a few of the wildest little pasture-fields that ever bordered a
wilderness of heath, or gave sustenance to a flock of grey moorland
sheep, with their little mossy faced lambs — they clung to this scene, I
say, with a perfect enthusiasm of attachment. (Jane Eyre. Chapter 30)*

Right: East Riddlesden Hall, outside Keighley, is a manor house with a tithe barn. It
belongs to the National Trust and is open to
the public.

Jane Eyre appreciates the way Thornfield is part of its isolated setting.

*. . . advancing on to the lawn, I looked up and surveyed the front of the
mansion. It was three stories high, of proportions not vast though
considerable; a gentleman's manor house, not a nobleman's seat:
battlements round the top gave it a picturesque look. Its grey front stood
out well from the background of a rookery, whose cawing tenants were
now on the wing. (Jane Eyre. Chapter 11)*

Finding no help in village or farm, Jane turns back to the moors in despair.

I saw I had strayed far from the village: it was quite out of sight. The very cultivation surrounding it had disappeared. I had, by cross-ways and bypaths, once more drawn near the tract of moorland; and now, only a few fields, almost as wild and unproductive as the heath from which they were scarcely reclaimed, lay between me and the dusky hill. (Jane Eyre. Chapter 28)

Looking towards Scar Hill over Haworth Moor.

'wuthering' being a significant provincial adjective, descriptive of the atmospheric tumult to which its station is exposed in stormy weather. Pure bracing ventilation they must have up there at all times, indeed. One may guess the power of the north wind blowing over the edge by the excessive slant of a few stunted firs at the end of the house, and by a gaunt range of thorns all stretching their limbs one way, as if craving alms of the sun. (Wuthering Heights. Chapter 1).

21

The wild heath has great beauty for Jane Eyre.

. . . my eye feasted on the outline of swell and sweep — on the wild colouring communicated to ridge and dell by moss, by heathbell, by flower-sprinkled turf, by brilliant bracken, and mellow granite crag. (Jane Eyre. Chapter 30)

Left: Haworth Moor with Top Withens on the horizon, south-west of Haworth.

Below: Whitestone Clough in the Worth Valley, west of Haworth.

The heather slopes of Sladen Beck on
Haworth Moor.

In *Wuthering Heights* perfect happiness is seen in terms of moorland scenery by the young
Linton Heathcliff and Cathy Linton.

24

Lying from morning till evening on a bank of heath in the middle of the moors, with the bees humming dreamily about among the bloom, and the larks singing high up overhead, and the blue sky and bright sun shining steadily and cloudlessly. (Wuthering Heights. Chapter 24)

25

Above: Stones on Grassington Moor, the southern limb of the Yorkshire Dales National Park.

Right: Ponden Clough on Haworth Moor with Ponden Kirk on the horizon, the 'Pennistow Crags' of *Wuthering Heights*.

The harshness of this unspoilt landscape is emphasised by the rocks and crags that appear in Emily Brontë's work.

. . . a bright, frosty afternoon, the ground bare, and the road hard and dry. I came to a stone where the highway branches off on to the moor at your left hand — a rough sand-pillar . . . (Wuthering Heights. Chapter 11)

The abrupt descent of Peniston Crags particularly attracted her notice especially when the setting sun shone on it and the topmost heights, and the whole extent of landscape besides lay in shadow. I explained that they were bare masses of stone, with hardly enough earth in their clefts to nourish a stunted tree. (Wuthering Heights. Chapter 18)

Previous page: Sheep on Haworth Moor.

Shirley compares the grandeur and loneliness of the Scottish highlands with her native Yorkshire moors.

. . . a district traversed one long afternoon, on a sultry but sunless day in summer: they journeyed from noon till sunset, over what seemed a boundless waste of deep heath, and nothing had they seen but wild sheep; nothing heard but the cries of wild birds. (Shirley. Chapter 12)

Right: Crossroads Mill, recently demolished above the Worth Valley, near Keighley.

But already nineteenth-century industrialisation is seen encroaching on the untamed heath in *Shirley*, as the hero rebuilds and extends his mill.

The other day I passed up the Hollow, which tradition says was once green and lone, and wild; and there I saw the manufacturer's day-dreams embodied in substantial stone and brick and ashes — the cinder-black highway, the cottages, and the cottage-gardens; there I saw a mighty mill, and a chimney, ambitious as the tower of Babel. (Shirley. Chapter 37)

Complete solitude is a comfort in Jane's disillusion with human beings.

There are great moors behind and on each hand of me; there are waves of mountains far beyond that deep valley at my feet. The population here must be thin, and I see no passengers on these roads. . . . (Jane Eyre. Chapter 28)

Looking west across Haworth Moor with the
Upper Worth Valley seen in the distance.

Left: Ponden Kirk. The rock out-crop is situated near Ponden Hall which is reputed to be the model for 'Thrushcross Grange' in *Wuthering Heights*.

Above: The view west across Haworth Moor with the heather in bloom.

Escaping from her deception by Rochester, Jane seeks refuge in the depths of wild Nature.

I struck straight into the heath; I held on to a hollow I saw deeply furrowing the brown moorside; I waded knee-deep in its dark growth; I turned with its turnings, and finding a moss-blackened granite crag in a hidden angle, I sat down under it. High banks of moor were about me; the crag protected my head: the sky was over that. (Jane Eyre. Chapter 28)

Left: Looking down Trow Gill, on the western fringe of the Yorkshire Dales.

Above: Brink Ends Farm on the moors above Wycoller in the Forest of Trawden. Wycoller village, centre of the County Park, includes 'Ferndean Manor' which was Rochester's home in *Jane Eyre*.

To Jane, the sense of space and distance symbolises a freedom to which she longs to escape.

My eyes passed all other objects to rest on those most remote, the blue peaks. It was those I longed to surmount; all within their boundary of rock and heath seemed prison ground, exile limits. I traced the white road winding round the base of one mountain, and vanishing in a gorge between two. How I longed to follow it further! (Jane Eyre. Chapter 10)

37

Above: Haymaking in the Worth Valley.

Right: Looking east across a windswept Haworth Moor with dry-stone walls, a common feature of the area.

... rocking in a rustling green tree, with a west wind blowing, and bright white clouds flitting rapidly above, and not only larks, but throstles and blackbirds, and linnets, and cuckoos pouring out music on every side, and the moors seen at a distance, broken into cool, dusky dells, but close by great swells of long grass undulating in waves, the breeze, and woods and sounding water, and the whole world awake and wild with joy. (Wuthering Heights. Chapter 24)

'The restless world of water'

Previous page: 'Brontë Bridge' on the route
from Haworth to Top Withens.

Right: Sladen Beck on Haworth Moor.

Charlotte Brontë told a school friend that as a girl she used to sit on a stone in a stream like the
child Jane Eyre.

*My favourite seat was a smooth and broad stone, rising white and dry
from the very middle of the beck, and only to be got at by wading
through the water; a feat I accomplished barefoot. The stone was just
broad enough to accommodate, comfortably, another girl and me. . . .
(Jane Eyre. Chapter 9)*

Overleaf: Eastergate Bridge on an old pack-
horse road leading over Marsden Moor in
the Colne Valley, West Yorkshire.

The same stream lies alongside Jane's way to the village.

*towards the close of a pleasant autumn day I found myself afoot on the
road to Lowton. A picturesque track it was, by the way; lying along the
side of the beck and through the sweetest curves of the dale; (Jane Eyre.
Chapter 10)*

The Brontë sisters often describe both the sound and appearance of water. Charlotte's 'professor' bids farewell to England beside a brimming river.

a sound of full-flowing water alone pervaded the air, for the river was deep and abundant, swelled by the melting of a late snow. I stood awhile, leaning over a wall; and looking down at the current: I watched the rapid rush of its waves. (The Professor. Chapter 5)

Left: Scaleber Force near Settle, North Yorkshire.

Below: The River Wharfe at the Strid, Bolton Abbey, in the Yorkshire Dales National Park.

Above: Northcliffe Woods, Bradford.   *Right*: Bluebells in woodland, Worth Valley.

Usually Charlotte associates water with freedom, Nature and solitude.

Here, the opposing sides of the glen approaching each other, and becoming clothed with brushwood and stunted oaks, formed a wooded ravine; at the bottom of which ran the mill-stream, in broken unquiet course, struggling with many stones, chafing against rugged banks, fretting with gnarled tree-roots, foaming, gurgling, battling as it went. Here when you had wandered half a mile from the mill, you found a sense of deep solitude; found it in the shade of unmolested trees; received it in the singing of many birds, for which that shade made a home. This was no trodden way: the freshness of the woodflowers attested that foot of man seldom pressed them; the abounding wild-roses looked as if they budded, bloomed and faded under the watch of solitude, as in a sultan's harem. Here you saw the sweet azure of the blue-bells, and recognised in pearl-white blossoms, spangling the grass, an humble type of some star-lit spot. (Shirley. Chapter 29)

Above: 'Brontë Falls', a small waterfall only spectacular after heavy rain.

Previous page: Blake Dean where Hebden Water and Alcomden Water meet under the edge of Widdop Moor, south-west of Haworth.

Centre: Lumb Falls and Bridge on Crimsworth Beck, at the foot of Cock Hill Moor, near Hebden Bridge.

Right: River Tees above High Force.

At the other extreme, Emily describes the general wetness of rainy, hilly countryside.

The rainy night had ushered in a misty morning, half frost, half drizzle, and temporary brooks crossed our path, gurgling from the uplands....(Wuthering Heights. Chapter 23)

Above left: A swollen moorland stream at Ponden Kirk.

Above right: The River Worth near Ponden Kirk.

Thus St. John Rivers is unwise in proposing a marriage of restraint and convention in a setting of freeflowing water and wild moorland!

... *a sort of pass, beyond which the beck rushed down a waterfall; and where, still a little further, the mountain shook off turf and flower, had only heath for raiment and crag for gem — where it exaggerated the wild to the savage, and exchanged the fresh for the frowning — where it guarded the forlorn hope of solitude, and a last refuge for silence. (Jane Eyre. Chapter 34)*

Forests, glades and wood-giants

Previous page: Heaton Wood near Shipley, Airedale.

Above: Woodland at Otley Chevin, West Yorkshire.

Left: River in spring near Hebden Bridge.

Although Charlotte seems to place woodland in the unhealthier areas of *Jane Eyre* such as Lowood and Ferndean manor, in *Shirley* on the other hand she celebrates the beauty and vital power of trees and forest. Even *Wuthering Heights* has its blossom and fruit.

59

Above left: Ivy growing on the mossy bark of
a tree-giant, Carleton Village, near Skipton.

I know groups of trees that ravish the eye with their perfect, picture-like effects: rude oak, delicate birch, glossy beech, clustered in contrast; and ash trees stately as Saul, standing isolated, and superannuated wood-giants clad in bright shrouds of ivy. (Shirley. Chapter 12)

Centre: Autumn trees bathed in early morning sun, Lister Park, Bradford.

Above right: Autumn beech trees at Hardcastle Crags, part of the National Trust valley near Hebden Bridge, West Yorkshire.

I know where we could get nuts in nutting time; I know where wild strawberries abound; I know certain lonely, quite untrodden glades, carpeted with strange mosses, some yellow as if gilded, some a sober grey, carpeted gem-green. (Shirley. Chapter 12)

Even within a very short distance of the manor house, you could see nothing of it, so thick and dark grew the timber of the gloomy wood about it. Iron gates between granite pillars showed me where to enter, and passing through them, I found myself at once in the twilight of close ranked trees. There was a grass-grown track descending the forest aisle between hoar and knotty shafts and under branched arches . . . all was interwoven stem, columnar trunk, dense summer foliage, — no opening anywhere. (Jane Eyre. Chapter 37)

Right: Sunrise near Heaton Royds, Bradford.

Previous page, left: Autumn trees in Lister Park, by Cartwright Hall, Bradford.

Previous page, right: Near Netherside Hall in Upper Wharfedale, Yorkshire.

Overleaf: Sunlight seen through the woodland mist at Shipley, West Yorkshire.

Above: Heaton Wood.

The trees are huge and old. When you stand at their roots, the summits seem in another region: the trunks remain still and firm as pillars, while the boughs sway to every breeze. In the deepest calm their leaves are never quite hushed, and in high wind a flood rushes — a sea thunders above you. (Shirley. Chapter 12)

Romantic hills, peaceful valleys

Above: Apple blossom in spring.   *Right*: Autumn apple trees with windfalls.

Previous page: Looking up Crimsworth Dean
towards Cock Hill Moor, near Haworth.

Not all the Brontë landscapes are harsh and primitive – some accommodate cultivation and man-made improvement.

We were in April then. The weather was sweet and warm, the grass as green as showers and sun could make it, and the two dwarf apple-trees near the southern walls in full bloom. (Wuthering Heights. Chapter 34)

On a mellow evening in September I was coming from the garden with a heavy basket of apples which I had been gathering. It had got dusk, and the moon looked over the high wall of the court, causing undefined shadows to lurk in the corners of the numerous projecting portions of the building. (Wuthering Heights. Chapter 10)

Overleaf, main picture: The view from Burtasett, Wensleydale, North Yorkshire.

Overleaf, bottom right: Kingcups in full flower.

Overleaf, top right: Looking towards Heptonstall Church from Pecket Well with Stoodley Pike on the horizon, a monument to mark the end of the Napoleonic Wars in 1814.

In *Shirley* village life is shown with its share of spring pleasures among the darker seasons of anxiety or struggle.

they looked down on the deep valley robed in May raiment; on varied meads, some pearled with daisies and some golden with king-cups; today all this young verdure smiled clear in sunlight; transparent emerald and amber gleams played over it. (Shirley. Chapter 12)

Right: Cragg Church in Cragg Vale, West Yorkshire.

Thornfield unites the qualities of pleasant solitude and friendly human society.

Farther off were hills; not so lofty as those round Lowood, nor so craggy, nor so like barriers of separation from the living world; but yet quiet and lonely hills enough, and seeming to embrace Thornfield with a seclusion I had not expected to find existent so near the stirring locality of Millcote. A little hamlet, whose roofs were blent with trees, straggled up the side of one of these hills; the church of the district stood nearer Thornfield: its old tower-top looked over a knoll between the house and gates. (Jane Eyre. Chapter 11)

Left: The upper lake in Bretton Park, West Yorkshire. The park is now the home of an outdoor sculpture museum.

Above: Hollywell Green Deer Park, near Halifax. Emily Brontë taught at Low Hill School Halifax for a short time.

Anne, like Charlotte, gave qualified praise to the grounds of houses such as those where they had lived in their governess days.

the park was spacious and beautiful, chiefly on account of its magnificent old trees, its stately herds of deer, its broad sheet of water, and the ancient woods that stretched beyond it; for there was no broken ground to give variety to the landscape, and but very little of that undulating swell which adds so greatly to the charm of park scenery. (Agnes Grey. Chapter 22)

He strayed down a walk edged with box, with apple-trees, pear-trees, and cherry-trees on one side, and a border on the other full of all sorts of old-fashioned flowers, stocks, sweet-williams, primroses, pansies, mingled with southernwood, sweet-briar, and various fragrant herbs. They were fresh now as a succession of April showers and gleams, followed by a lovely spring morning, could make them: the sun was just entering the dappled east, and his light illumined the wreathed and dewy orchard-trees and shone down the quiet walks under them. (Jane Eyre. Chapter 20)

An English country garden in springtime.

In the walled garden of Norton Conyers, near Ripon.

The Old Silent Inn, Worth Valley, in midsummer.

Above: Luddenden Dean, West Yorkshire.

Right: The evening sun slanting across a summer landscape after harvest in the Worth Valley.

The sun shines on Jane Eyre in her happier period at Thornfield.

A splendid Midsummer shone over England: skies so pure, suns so radiant as were then seen in long succession, seldom favour, even singly, our wave-girt land. It was as if a band of Italian days had come from the South, like a flock of glorious passenger birds, and lighted to rest them on the cliffs of Albion. The hay was all got in; the fields round Thornfield were green and shorn; the roads white and baked; the trees were in their dark prime; hedge and wood, full-leaved and deeply tinted, contrasted well with the sunny hue of the cleared meadows between. (Jane Eyre. Chapter 23)

Winter Landscapes

Left: A wintry sunset over Malham Moor, North Yorkshire.

Above: Ponden Clough under light snow, West Yorkshire.

Previous page: Heptonstall Church and Stoodley Pike from Pecket Well, Calderdale.

Winter, long and trying in places like high unsheltered Haworth, plays a large part in the novels. Wuthering Heights baffles the southerner Lockwood with its bleak, uncompromising winter weather.

. . . the whole hill-back was one billowy, white ocean; the swells and falls not indicating corresponding rises and depressions in the ground: many pits, at least, were filled to a level; and entire ranges of mounds, the refuse of the quarries, blotted out from the chart which my yesterday's walk left pictured in my mind. (Wuthering Heights. Chapter 3)

Left: Clear, sharp weather on a winter's day on Haworth Moor. The dry stone wall made from local grit-stone can be clearly picked out against the snow.

Above: Haworth Moor at twilight with the full moon rising over the snow.

Winter returns treacherously, teaching the characters in the novels not to be too optimistic!

That Friday made the last of our fine days for a month. In the evening the weather broke; the wind shifted from south to north-west and brought rain first, and then sleet and snow. On the morrow one could hardly imagine that there had been three weeks of summer. (Wuthering Heights. Chapter 17)

Above: The winter sun setting on Haworth Moor.

Previous page: Sheep on Haworth Moor in winter.

To the young and weak at Lowood, winter brings not beauty but threat and suffering.

How different had this scene looked when I viewed it laid out beneath the iron sky of winter, stiffened in frost, shrouded with snow! — when mists as chill as death wandered to the impulse of east winds along those purple peaks, and rolled down 'ing' and holm till they blended with the frozen fog of the beck! (Jane Eyre. Chapter 9)

Moonrise over Malham Moor, near Malham Tarn, North Yorkshire.

... the primroses and crocuses were hidden under windy drifts, the larks were silent, the young leaves of the early trees smitten and blackened, and dreary, and chill, and dismal that morrow did creep over. (Wuthering Heights. Chapter 17)

Glusburn Moor near Stone Gappe, Lothersdale. Charlotte Brontë was for a time governess at 'Stone Gappe' and later used the house as her model for Gateshead Hall in *Jane Eyre*.

The feelings of the child Jane Eyre are mirrored in her surroundings.

I leaned against a gate, and looked into an empty field where no sheep were feeding, where the short grass was nipped and blanched. It was a very grey day; a most opaque sky, 'onding on snaw', canopied all; then flakes fell at intervals, which settled on the hard path and on the hoary lea without melting. (Jane Eyre. Chapter 4)

Left: The full moon rising over Ponden Reservoir in the Worth Valley.

Above: Lower Laithe Reservoir, seen from Stanbury.

Yet as Jane grows more independent, she finds pleasure in winter and solitude.

On the hilltop above me sat the rising moon; pale yet as a cloud, but brightening momently; she looked over Hay, which, half lost in trees, sent up a blue smoke from its few chimneys; it was yet a mile distant but in the absolute hush I could hear plainly its thin murmurs of life. My ear, too, felt the flow of currents; in what dales and depths I could not tell; but there were many hills beyond Hay, and doubtless many becks threading their passes. That evening calm betrayed alike the tinkle of the nearest streams, the sough of the most remote. (Jane Eyre. Chapter 12)

Previous page: A winter sunset over fields at Stanbury in the Worth Valley, West Yorkshire.

Hard and cold, the atmosphere that meets Lockwood at Wuthering Heights is intended to make the stranger feel unwelcome. However, the inquisitive Lockwood does not heed the warning.

Hepstonstall Church and village with the snow-clad Pennine Hills on the horizon.

On that bleak hill-top the earth was hard with a black frost and the air made me shiver through every limb. (Wuthering Heights. Chapter 2)

Mist, cloud and sunsets

A moorland landscape, uninterrupted by buildings or woodland, gives scope for magnificent sunsets – all the novels introduce fiery evening skies, usually marking periods of happiness and fulfilment.

Previous page: Elslack Moor over Lothersdale where Stone Gappe is situated. Lothersdale, north-west of Haworth is on the Pennine Way.

Below: A spectacular red dawn over Haworth Moor.

... rambling leisurely along, with the glow of a sinking sun behind, and the mild glory of a rising moon in front — one fading, and the other brightening, as I quitted the park, and climbed the stony by-road branching off to Mr. Heathcliff's dwelling. Before I arrived in sight of it, all that remained of day was a beamless amber light along the west: but I could see every pebble on the path, and every blade of grass, by that splendid moon. (Wuthering Heights. Chapter 32)

The footpath to the Brontë Waterfalls on Haworth Moor with a radiant evening sky.

Charlotte is anxious to convey the exact shade and nuance of this subtle colouring of the winter sky.

'I know how the heath would look on such a day,' said Caroline; 'purple-black: a deeper shade of the sky tint, and that would be livid.' 'Yes – quite livid, with brassy edges to the clouds, and here and there a white gleam, more ghastly than the lurid tinge, which as you looked at it, you momentarily expected would kindle into blinding lightning.' (Shirley. Chapter 12)

Clouds over Haworth Moor.

Above: Autumn sunset with sheep grazing in the pastures of Wycoller Dean, west of Haworth.

Right: The Dales' mountain summits of Ingleborough and Pen-y-Gwent stand out against the summer sunset, seen from the top of Cock Hill Moor, near Haworth.

It was now the sweetest hour of the twenty-four: 'day its fervid fires had wasted', and dew fell cool on panting plain and scorched summit. Where the sun had gone down in simple state; pure of the pomp of clouds – spread a solemn purple, burning with the light of red jewels and furnace flame at one point, on one hill-peak, and extending high and wide, soft and still softer, over half heaven. The east had its own charm of fine, deep blue, and its own modest gem, a rising and solitary star: soon it would boast the moon; but she was yet beneath the horizon. (Jane Eyre. Chapter 23)

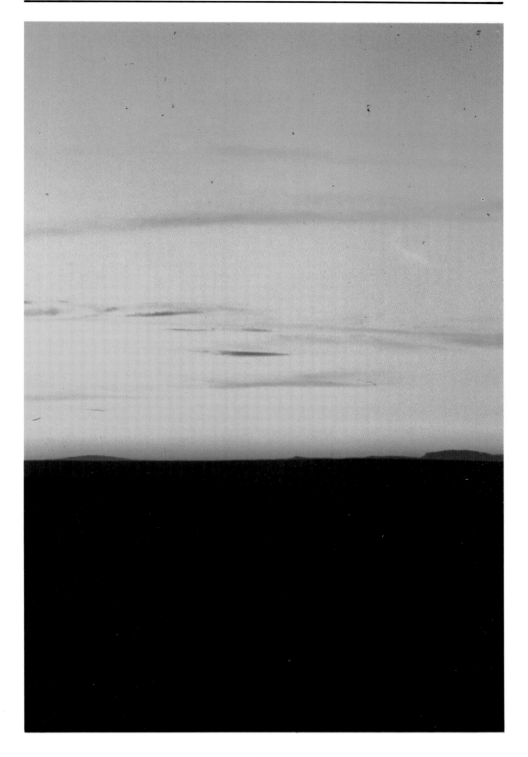

Dusk over a snowy landscape on Haworth Moor.

A calm day had settled into a crystalline evening; the world wore a North Pole colouring: all its lights and tints looked like the 'reflets' of white, or violet, or pale green gems. The hills wore a lilac-blue; the setting sun had purple in its red; the sky was ice, all silvered azure; when the stars rose, they were of white crystal — not gold; grey; or cerulean, or faint emerald hues — cool, pure and transparent — tinged the mass of the landscape. (Shirley. Chapter 32)

Above: Cloud formations over Haworth Moor.

On an afternoon in October or the beginning of November, a fresh, watery afternoon, when the turf and paths were rustling with moist withered leaves, and the cold blue sky was half hidden by clouds — dark grey streamers, rapidly mounting from the west and boding abundant rain . . . (Wuthering Heights. Chapter 22)

The evening was still and warm; close and sultry it even promised to become. Round the descending sun the clouds glowed purple: summer tints, rather Indian than English, suffused the horizon, and cast rosy reflections of hillside, house-front, tree-bole; on winding road, and undulating pasture-ground . . . the whole scene was solitary. (Shirley. Chapter 18)

Above: Sunset over the Worth Valley.

Charlotte at one time had ambitions to be an artist, and her sense of colour and form appears in her descriptions of unusual and transient effects of light and weather.

Previous page: Mist in the Worth Valley, near the small village of Stanbury, outside Haworth.

Below: High hills and steep valleys with lakes and reservoirs often give rise to the familiar Pennine mist. The morning mist is seen here in the Upper Worth Valley.

The hills seemed rolled in a sullen mist, and when the rain fell in whitening sheets, suddenly they were blotted from the prospect: they were washed from the world. (Shirley. Chapter 12)

The Brontë sisters studied the changes in their surroundings as the days and years went by. Emily's description of mist is detailed and precise as well as atmospheric.

. . . a window whose lattice lay back against the wall, and displayed, beyond the garden trees and the wild green park, the valley of Gimmerton with a long line of mist winding nearly to its top (for very soon after you pass the chapel, as you may have noticed, the sough that runs from the marshes joins a beck which follows the bend of the glen.) (Wuthering Heights. Chapter 10)

The spectacular cliffs at Filey, on the
east coast of Yorkshire.

*. . . the sight and the sound of the sea dashing against my promontory —
with no prodigious force, for the swell was broken by the tangled
seaweed and the unseen rocks beneath; otherwise I should soon have been
deluged with spray. But the tide was coming in; the water was rising;
the gulfs and lakes were filling; the straits were widening, it was time to
seek some safer footing . . . (Agnes Grey. Chapter 24)*

"... the tide was coming in; the water
was rising ..."

This is an autumn evening, wet and wild. There is only one cloud in the sky; but it curtains it from pole to pole. The wind cannot rest: it hurries sobbing over hills of sullen outline, colourless with twilight and mist. Rain has beat all day on that church-tower: it rises dark from the stony enclosure of its graveyard; the nettles, the long grass, and the tombs all drip with wet. (Shirley. Chapter 23)

Overleaf: The churchyard at Haworth where most of the Brontë family are buried.

Index of Books

General Index

Chronology

1777 Patrick Brontë is born in County Down.

1783 Maria Branwell (afterwards Mrs Brontë) born in Penzance.

1812 Patrick marries Maria Branwell.

1813 Maria Brontë is born at Hartshead, Yorkshire.

1815 8 February. Elizabeth Brontë is born at Hartshead.

1816 21 April. Charlotte Brontë is born at Thornton, Yorkshire.

1817 26 June. Patrick Branwell Brontë is born at Thornton.

1818 30 July. Emily Jane Brontë is born at Thornton.

1820 17 January. Anne Brontë is born at Thornton.
Patrick appointed to incumbency of Haworth; family moves there.

1821 Mrs Brontë dies.

1823 Rev. Patrick Brontë tries unsuccessfully to remarry.
Miss Elizabeth Branwell ('Aunt') moves to Haworth.

1824 Maria and Elizabeth Brontë go to Cowan Bridge Clergy Daughters' School (July).
Charlotte (August) and Emily (November) to Cowan Bridge.

1825 Maria and Elizabeth leave Cowan Bridge and die of TB.
Patrick fetches Charlotte and Elizabeth home.

1831 Charlotte goes to Miss Wooler's school at Roe Head.

1832 Charlotte leaves Roe Head.

1835 Emily is a pupil at Roe Head.
Branwell studies painting with William Robinson, a Leeds artist.

1836 Anne at Roe Head. Branwell plans to enter Royal Academy Schools in London, but does not. He opens a studio in Bradford and paints portraits, unsuccessfully.

1837 Emily becomes governess at a school near Halifax.

1839 Anne becomes governess with Mrs Ingham at Mirfield.
Charlotte becomes governess with Mrs Sidgwick at Stonegappe.

1840 Branwell becomes a tutor and then a railway clerk. Anne becomes governess at Thorp Green.

1841 Charlotte becomes governess with the Whites at Rawdon.

1842 Charlotte and Emily go to M. Heger's school in Brussels. 'Aunt' dies, so they return to Haworth.

1843 January. Charlotte returns to Brussels but leaves in December.
Branwell becomes tutor to the Robinsons at Thorp Green.

1845 Rev. A. B. Nicholls comes to Haworth.
Anne leaves Thorp Green. Branwell is dismissed. Charlotte chances on Emily's recent poems and proposes the publication of a joint volume.

1846 Publication of *Poems* by Currer, Ellis and Acton Bell. The three girls each write a novel. Emily's *Wuthering Heights* and Anne's *Agnes Grey* are accepted. Charlotte's *The Professor* is refused; she begins to write *Jane Eyre*.

1847 October. *Jane Eyre* published by Smith, Elder. Immediate success.
December. *Wuthering Heights* and *Agnes Grey* published together. Fail.

1848 July. Anne's *The Tenant of Wildfell Hall* published.
24 September. Branwell dies.
19 December. Emily dies.

1849 28 May. Anne dies.
26 October. *Shirley* published.

1853 28 January. *Villette* published.

1854 29 June. Charlotte marries The Rev. A. B. Nicholls.

1855 31 March. Charlotte dies.

1857 March. Mrs Gaskell's *Life of Charlotte Brontë* is published.
The Professor is published.

1861 7 June. Patrick Brontë dies.

1872 October. Publication of the first illustrated edition of the Brontë works.

1893 Foundation of the Brontë Society.

1928 Haworth Parsonage becomes the Brontë Parsonage Museum.